PIANO • VOCAL • GUITAR

ALVIN THE C_____RS

70's

80's

they're back.

FOX 2000 PICTURES and REGENCY ENTERPRISES PRESENT A BAGDASARIAN COMPANY PRODUCTION "ALVIN AND THE CHIPMUNKS" JASON LEE DAVID CROSS CAMERON RICHARDSON AND JUSTIN LONG MATTHEW GRAY GUBLER JESSE McCARTNEY MUSIC SUPERVISOR JULIANNE JORDAN MUSIC BY CHRISTOPHER LENNERTZ SONGS PRODUCED BY ALI DEE THEODORE VISUAL EFFECTS BY RHYTHM & HUES STUDIOS EDITED BY PETER BERGER, A.C.E. PRODUCTION DESIGNER RICHARD HOLLAND DIRECTOR OF PHOTOGRAPHY PETER LYONS COLLISTER, ASC EXECUTIVE PRODUCERS KAREN ROSENFELT ARNON MILCHAN MICHELE IMPERATO STABILE STEVE WATERMAN PRODUCED BY JANICE KARMAN ROSS BAGDASARIAN BASED UPON THE CHARACTERS "ALVIN AND THE CHIPMUNKS" CREATED BY ROSS BAGDASARIAN STORY BY JON VITTI SCREENPLAY BY JON VITTI AND WILL McROBB & CHRIS VISCARDI

ISBN 978-1-4234-5522-6

REGENCY   20th CENTURY FOX

HAL•LEONARD®
CORPORATION
7777 W. BLUEMOUND RD. P.O. BOX 13819 MILWAUKEE, WI 53213

Visit Hal Leonard Online at
www.halleonard.com

BAD DAY

Words and Music by
DANIEL POWTER

and I don't need _ no car - ryin' on. ___

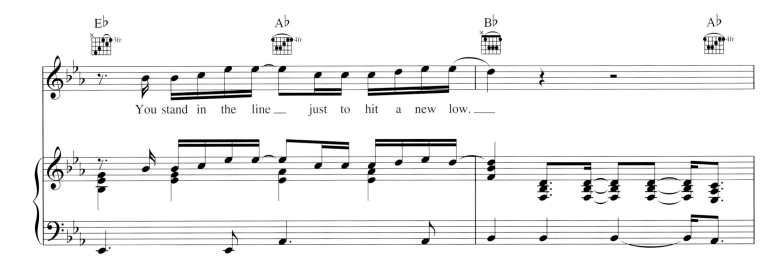

You stand in the line _ just to hit a new low. ___

You're fak - in' the smile _ with the cof - fee to go. _____

They tell me your life's _ been way _ off line. _ You've fall - en to piec - es ev - 'ry time _

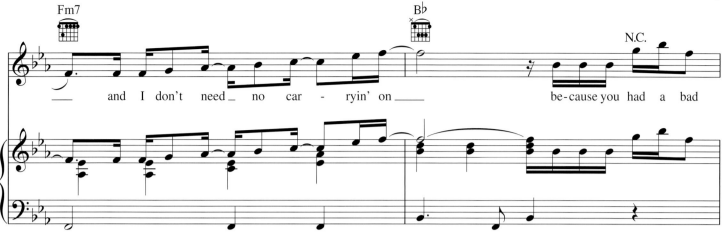

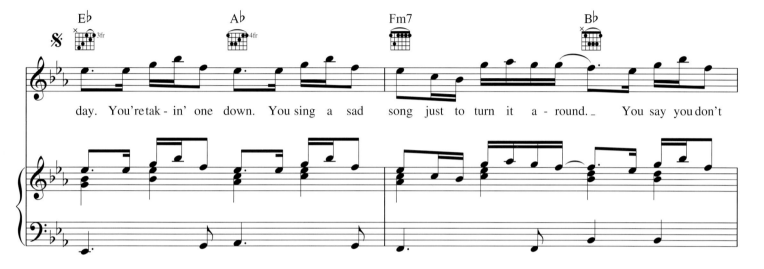

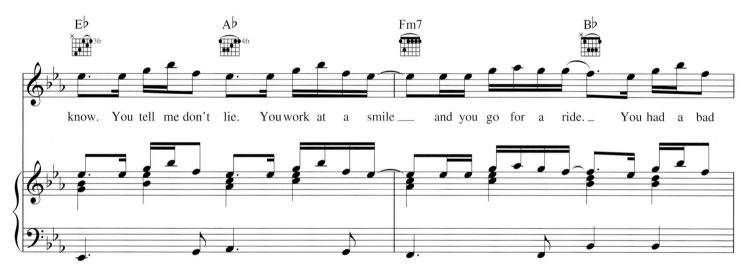

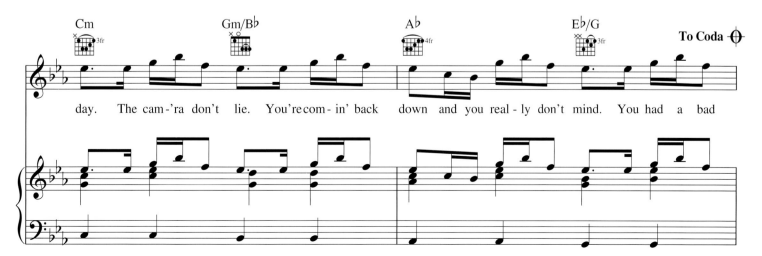

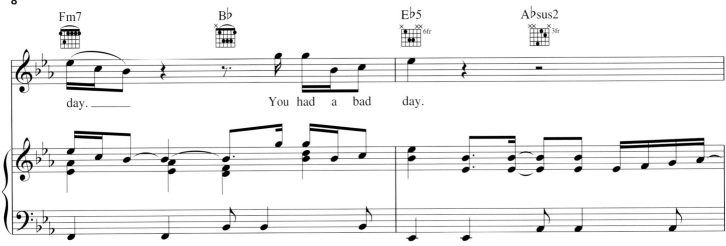

day. _____ You had a bad day.

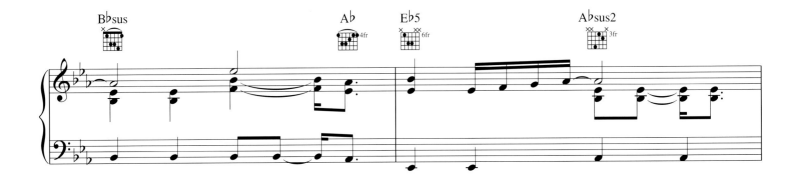

Well, you need a blue _ sky hol - i - day. _

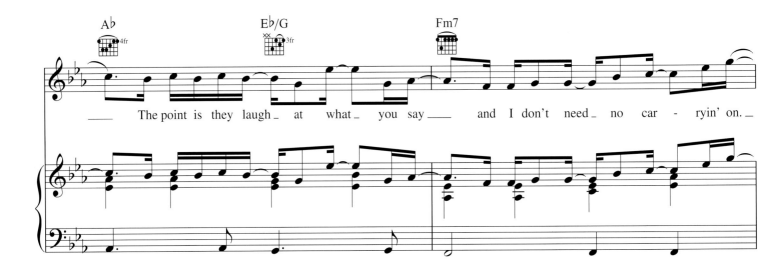

_____ The point is they laugh _ at what _ you say _____ and I don't need _ no car - ryin' on. _

So where is the pas - sion when you need it the most?_

_ Oh, ___ you and I. _____ You kick up the leaves_ and the mag - ic is lost_

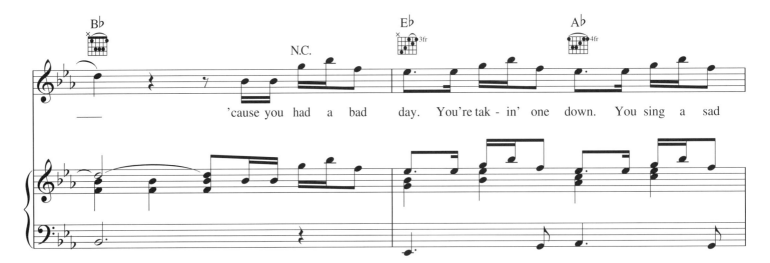

_ 'cause you had a bad day. You're tak - in' one down. You sing a sad

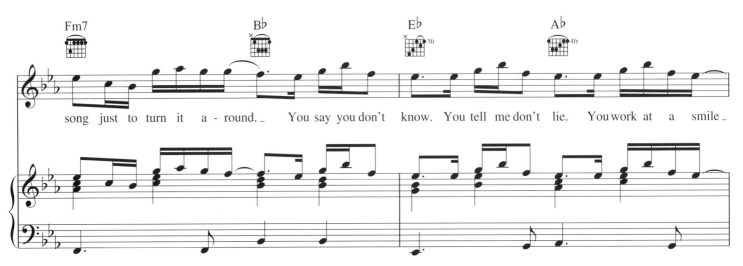

song just to turn it a - round._ You say you don't know. You tell me don't lie. You work at a smile_

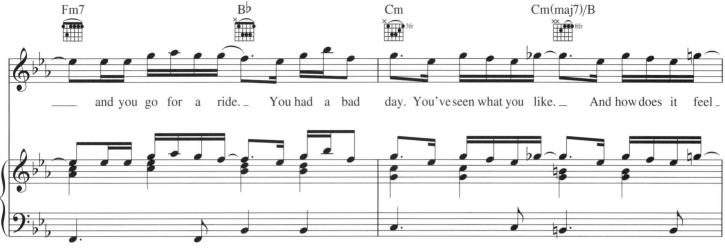

and you go for a ride. ___ You had a bad day. You've seen what you like. ___ And how does it feel ___

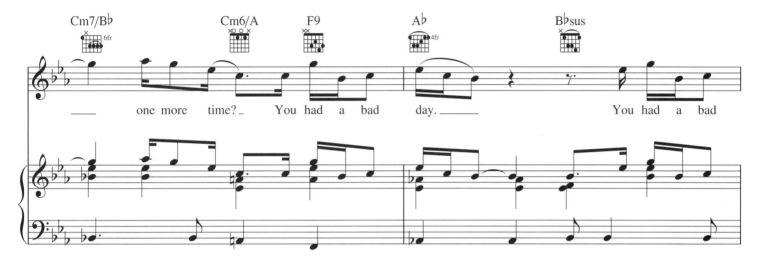

___ one more time? ___ You had a bad day. ___ You had a bad

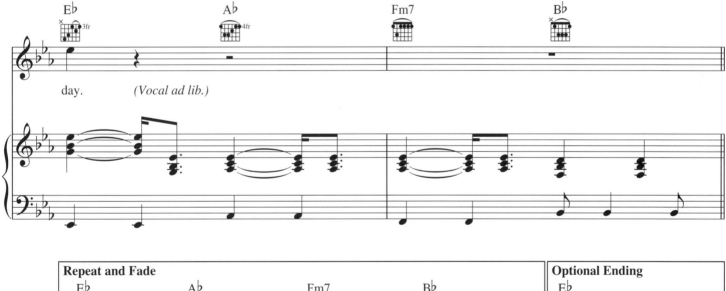

day. *(Vocal ad lib.)*

Repeat and Fade   **Optional Ending**

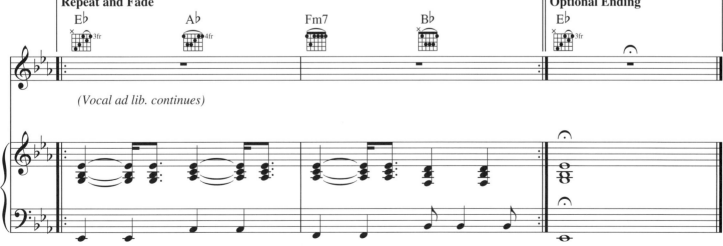

(Vocal ad lib. continues)

THE CHIPMUNK SONG

Words and Music by
ROSS BAGDASARIAN

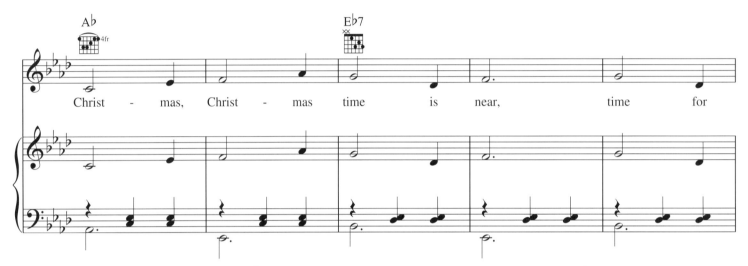

Christ - mas, Christ - mas time is near, time for

toys and time for cheer. We've been

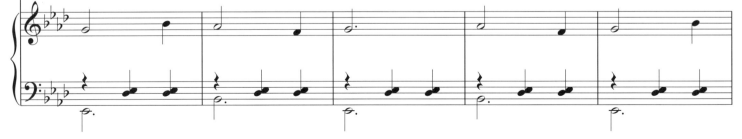

good, but we can't last. Hur - ry Christ - mas,

FOLLOW ME NOW

Words and Music by ALI THEODORE,
JOSEPH KATSAROS and SHEILA OWENS

This morn-ing I woke up and some-thing had changed. _

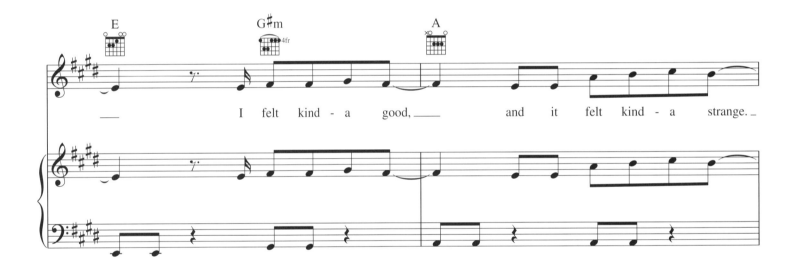

_ I felt kind-a good, _ and it felt kind-a strange. _

_ There's some-thing go-ing on here and may-be it's a

brand - new world, ___ or I'm just cra - zy in - sane. ___

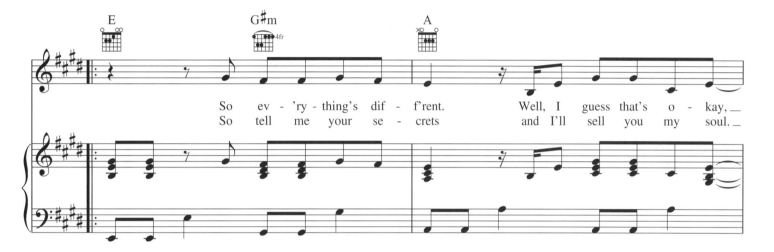

So ev - 'ry - thing's dif - f'rent. Well, I guess that's o - kay, ___
So tell me your se - crets and I'll sell you my soul. ___

___ 'cause those thoughts that used to hold ___ me down have all gone a - way. ___
___ There's a shov - el in my heart _____ and it's dig - ging a hole. ___

___ I feel like I could take on the world, ___ so come a -
___ The dev - il and the god in my head ___ are hav - ing

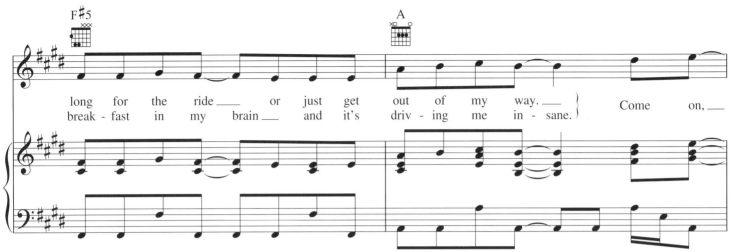

long for the ride ___ or just get out of my way. ___ Come on, ___
break - fast in my brain ___ and it's driv - ing me in - sane.

___ come on, ___ get up, ___ get up, ___ let's go, won't you fol - low me?

Come on, ___ come on, ___ get up, ___ get up, ___ let's

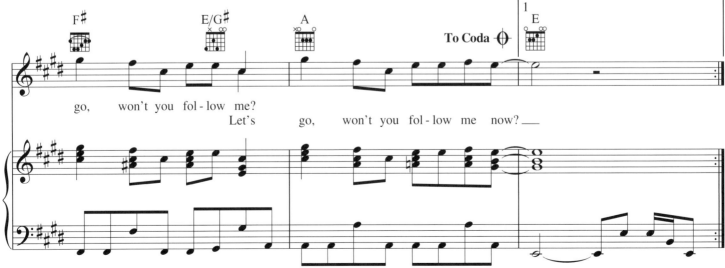

go, won't you fol - low me?
Let's go, won't you fol - low me now? ___

Ah, __ oh, __ ah, __ oh, __ ah, __ oh, __ ah. Ah, __ oh, __ ah, __ oh, __

__ ah, __ oh, __ ah. Ah, __ oh, __ ah, __ oh, __ ah, __ oh, __ ah. Let's

go, __ won't you fol - low me now? __

D.S. al Coda

Won't some-one fol - low me now? __ Won't some-one fol - low me now? __
Come on, __

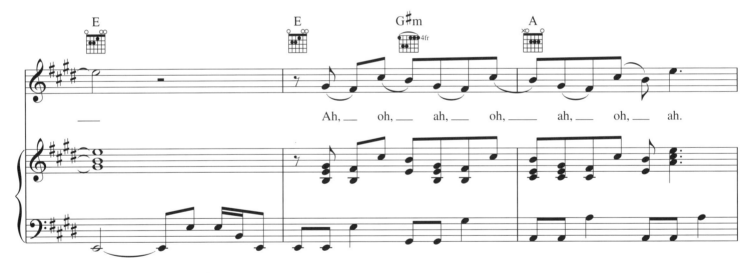

HOW WE ROLL

Words and Music by ALI THEODORE, JOSEPH KATSAROS,
ZACH DANZIGER and ALANA DAFONSECA

Urban groove

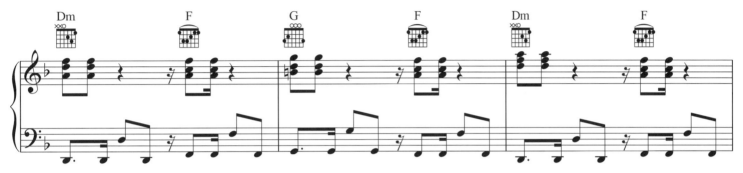

You know you've got it made when you drop the es-ca-lade for the drop top,
stay when you're al-ways get-ting paid and it won't stop,

iced out rock's hot, drop-ping dol-lars, la-dies hol-ler, hey, got to get that
nev-er will it won't stop, no___ mat-ter what___ they___ say, gon-na live the

cream. _____ You know you've got it made when they send in a pa-rade when you drop down.
dream. _____ You know you're here to stay when there ain't a thing to hate 'cause we that sick,

Pri - vate jet in town all for just one day, got to get that
ev - 'ry - bod - y sweet chip, got noth - ing to say, so we live the

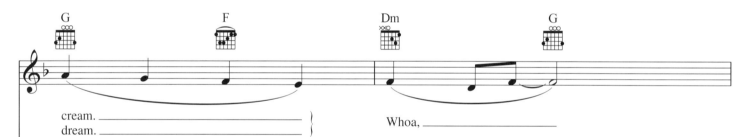

cream. _____ Whoa, _____
dream. _____

don't you know that's how we roll, _____

How we roll.

You know you're here to

Break it down, now.

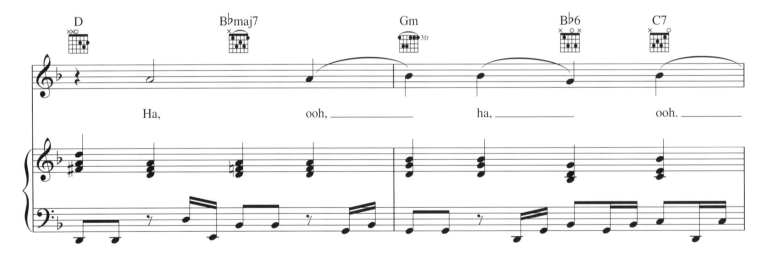

Ha, ooh, ha, ooh.

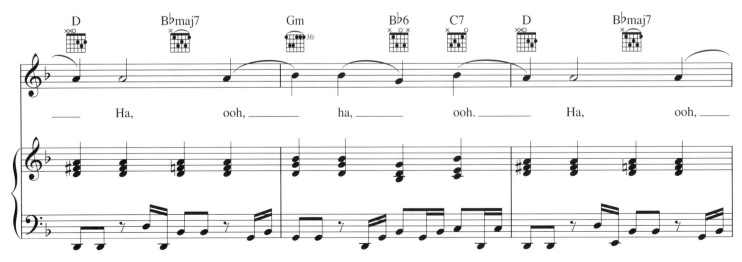

Ha, ooh, ha, ooh. Ha, ooh,

D.S. al Coda

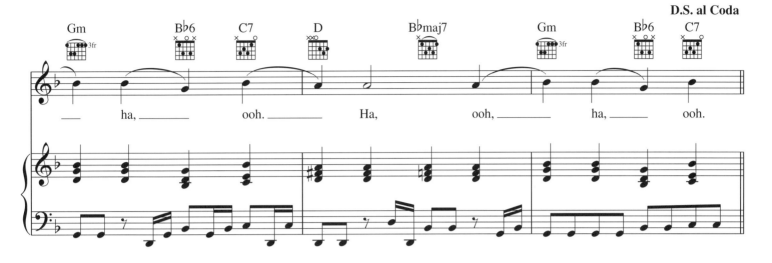

ha, _____ ooh. _____ Ha, ooh, _____ ha, _____ ooh.

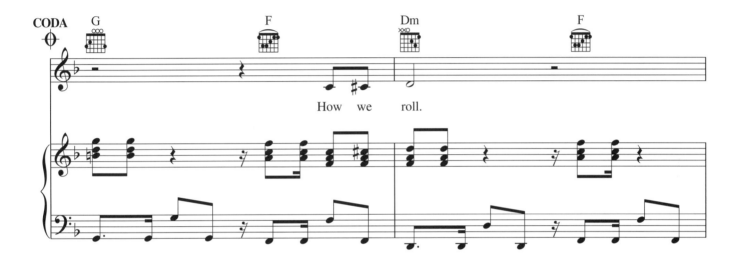

How we roll.

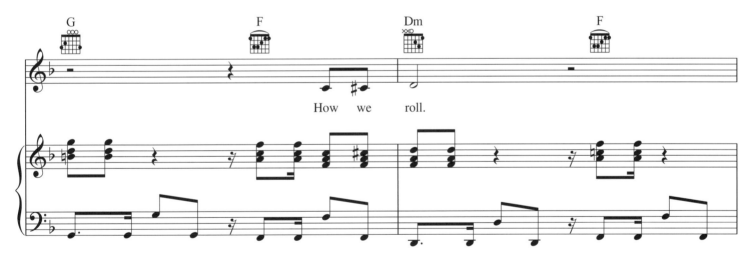

How we roll.

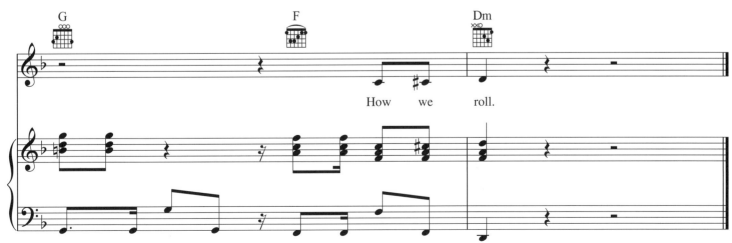

How we roll.

WITCH DOCTOR

Words and Music by
ROSS BAGDASARIAN

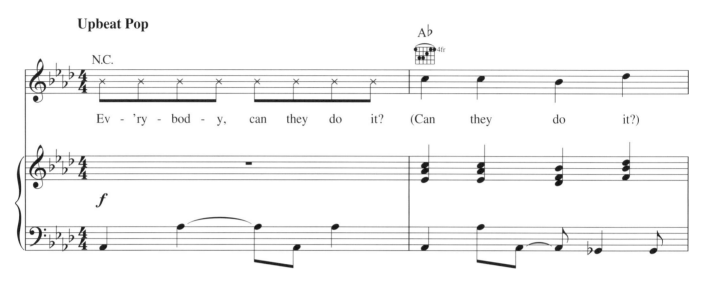

Upbeat Pop

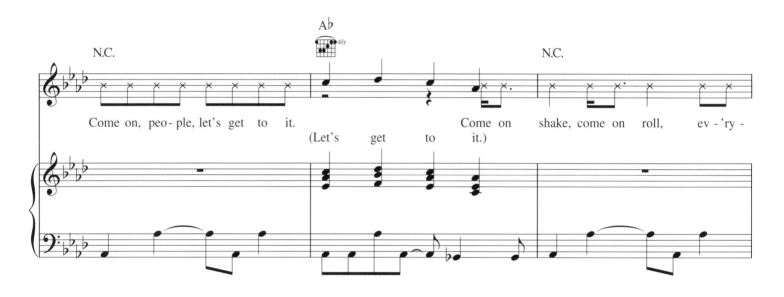

Ev-'ry-bod-y, can they do it? (Can they do it?)

Come on, peo-ple, let's get to it. (Let's get to it.) Come on shake, come on roll, ev-'ry-

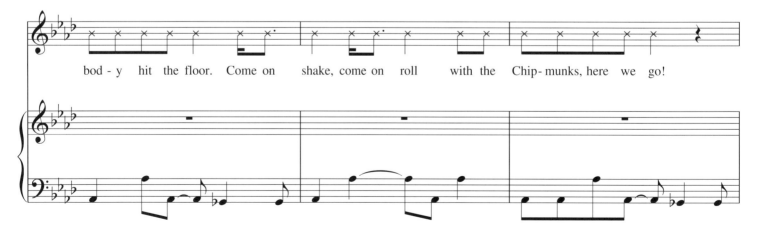

bod-y hit the floor. Come on shake, come on roll with the Chip-munks, here we go!

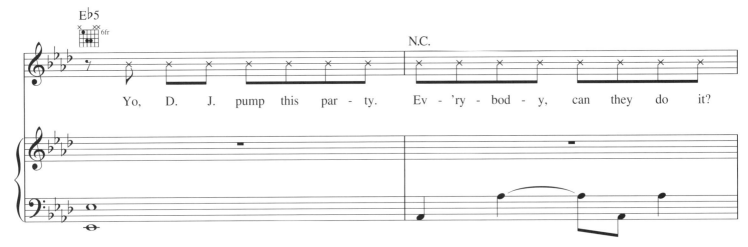

Yo, D. J. pump this par - ty. Ev - 'ry - bod - y, can they do it?

(Can they do it?) Come on, peo - ple, let's get to it.

(Let's get to it.) Come on shake, come on roll, ev - 'ry -

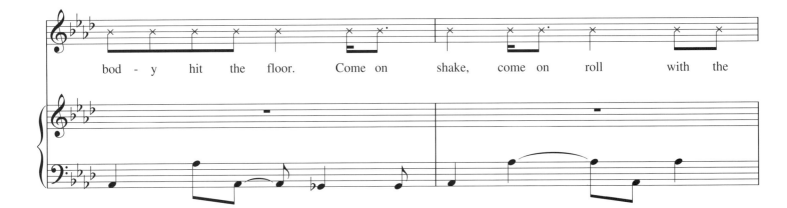

bod - y hit the floor. Come on shake, come on roll with the

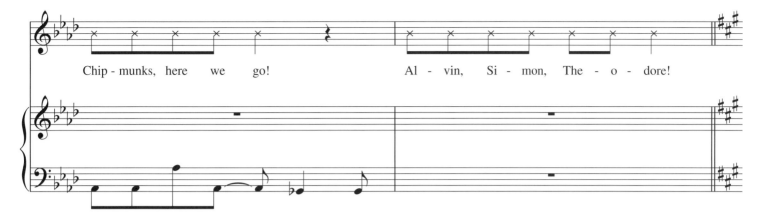

Chip - munks, here we go! Al - vin, Si - mon, The - o - dore!

A

I told the witch doc - tor you did - n't love me true._____

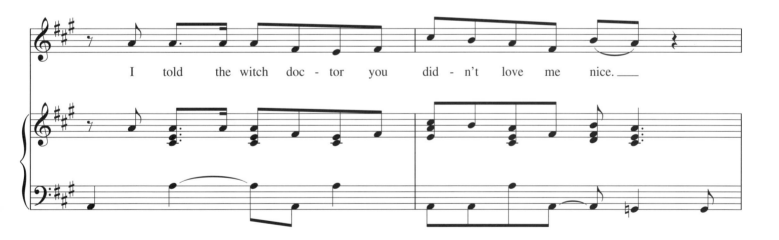

I told the witch doc - tor you did - n't love me nice.____

B

And then the witch doc - tor, he gave me this ad - vice. He said do you

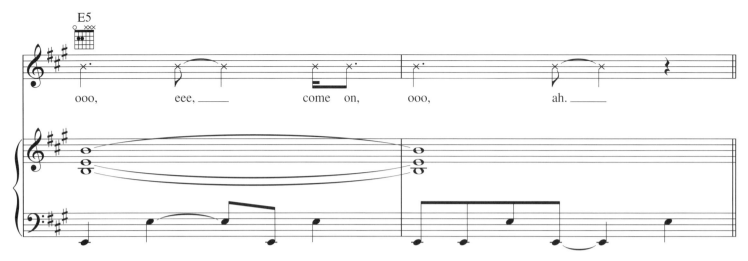

ooo, eee, _____ come on, ooo, ah. _____

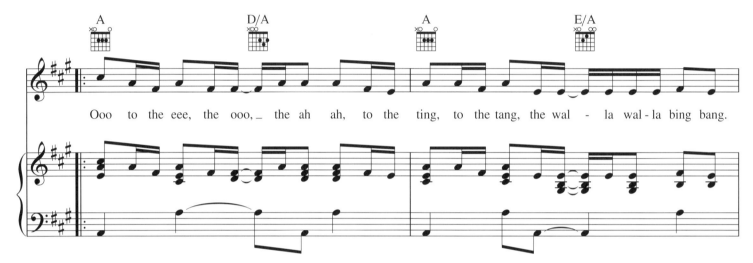

Ooo to the eee, the ooo, _ the ah ah, to the ting, to the tang, the wal - la wal - la bing bang.

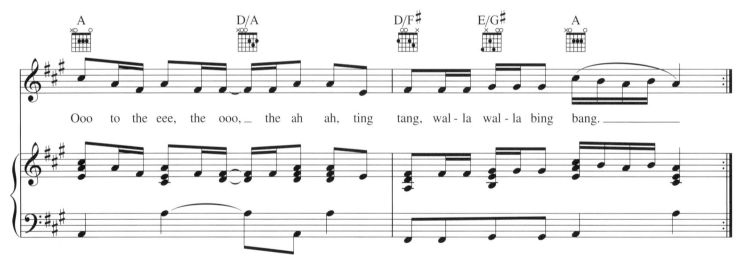

Ooo to the eee, the ooo, _ the ah ah, ting tang, wal - la wal - la bing bang. _____

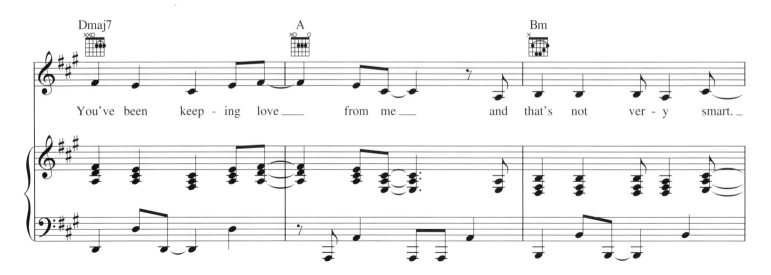

You've been keep - ing love _____ from me _____ and that's not ver - y smart. _

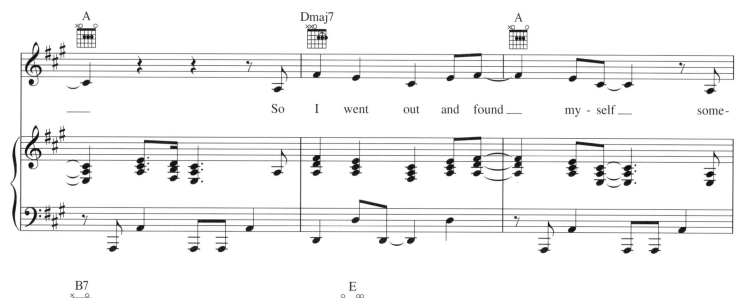

I know that you'll be ___ mine when I say this ___ to you. ___

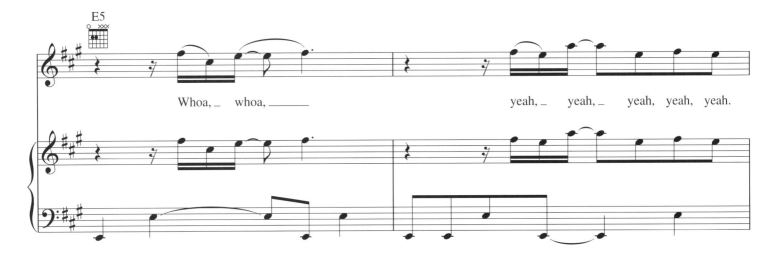

Whoa, ___ whoa, ___ yeah, ___ yeah, ___ yeah, yeah, yeah.

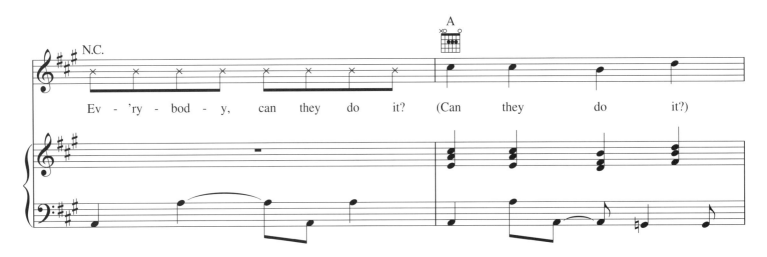

Ev - 'ry - bod - y, can they do it? (Can they do it?)

Come on, peo - ple, let's get to it. Come on
(Let's get to it.)

COME GET IT

Words and Music by ALI THEODORE,
ALANA DAFONSECA and AARON SANDLOFER

Syncopated groove

Heads are turn - in', boys are yearn - in', want to get up on us.

Pick - in' game, it's all the same when all the fel - las want us.

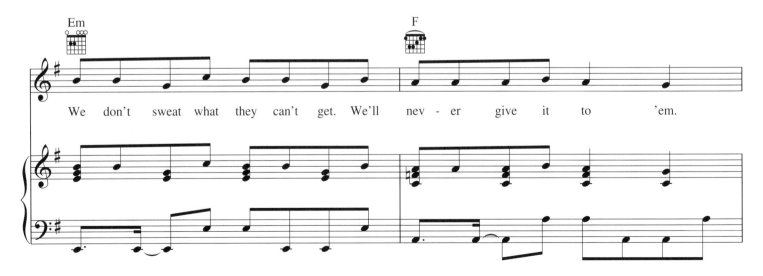

We don't sweat what they can't get. We'll nev - er give it to 'em.

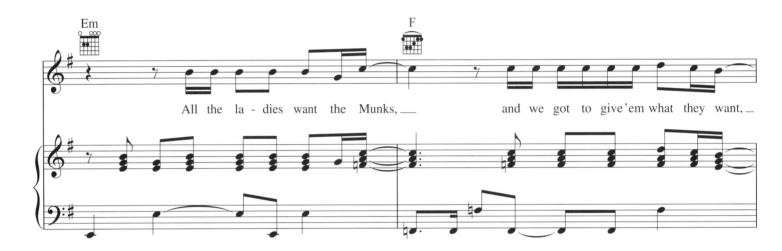

To Coda ⊕

Let's get this par - ty start - ed right, I'll keep you go - ing all

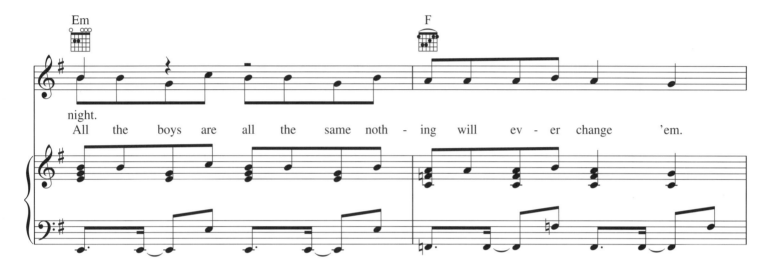

night.
All the boys are all the same noth - ing will ev - er change 'em.

They all want one thing and, girl, you know you'll nev - er tame 'em.

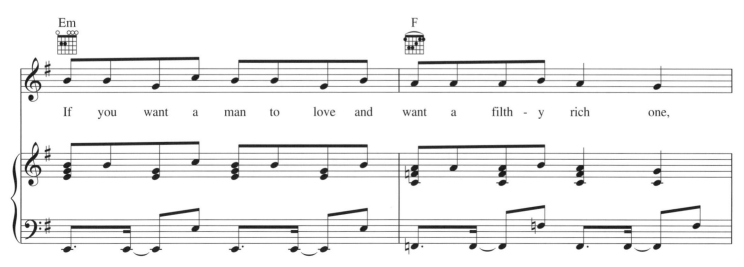

If you want a man to love and want a filth - y rich one,

then I know where you should go. 'Cause, girl, you want a Chip - munk! __

night, I'll keep you go-ing all __ night.
If you want a lit-tle bit of this and a lit-tle bit of that,

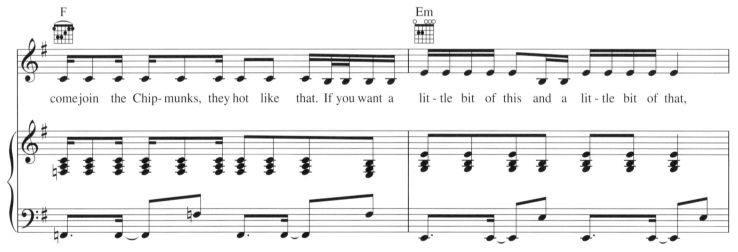

come join the Chip-munks, they hot like that. If you want a lit-tle bit of this and a lit-tle bit of that,

come to the Chip-munks, they hot like that. If you want a lit-tle bit of this and a lit-tle bit of that,

we just a three young broth - ers. But when we real-ly like to get to get to know __ you, that's when we

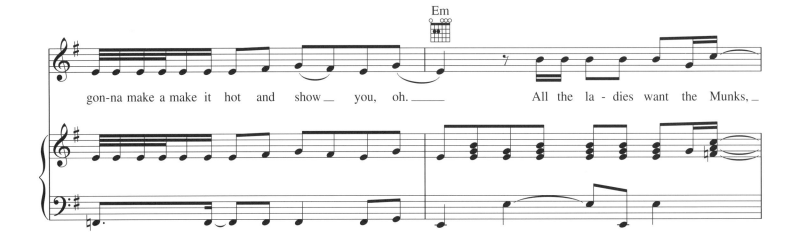

gon-na make a make it hot and show __ you, oh. __ All the la - dies want the Munks, __

__ and we got to give 'em what they want, __ when we're kick-ing it in the truck __

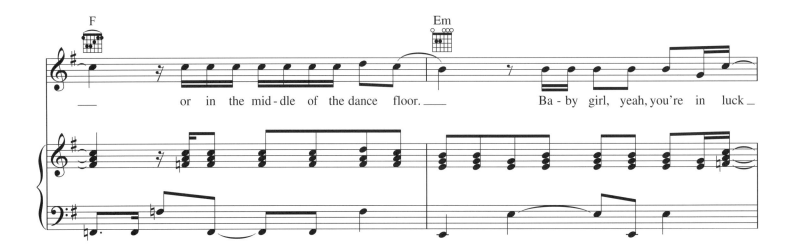

__ or in the mid-dle of the dance floor. __ Ba - by girl, yeah, you're in luck __

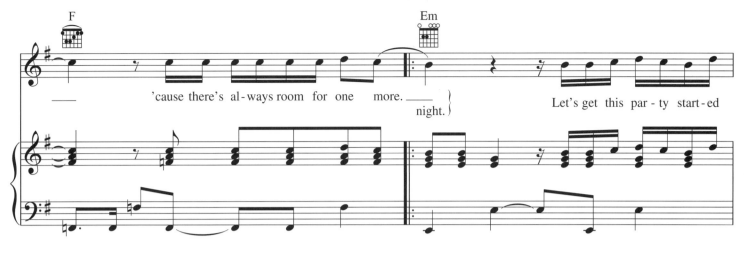

'cause there's al-ways room for one more. ___ night. Let's get this par-ty start-ed

right, I'll keep you go-ing all ___ night. Let's get this par-ty start-ed

right, I'll keep you go-ing all ___ right. Whoa, oh. ___

I'll keep you go-ing all ___ night.

THE CHIPMUNK SONG
(DeeTown Rock Mix)

Words and Music by
ROSS BAGDASARIAN

Punk Pop

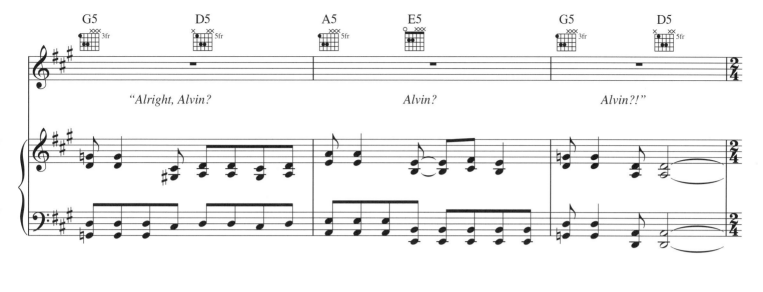

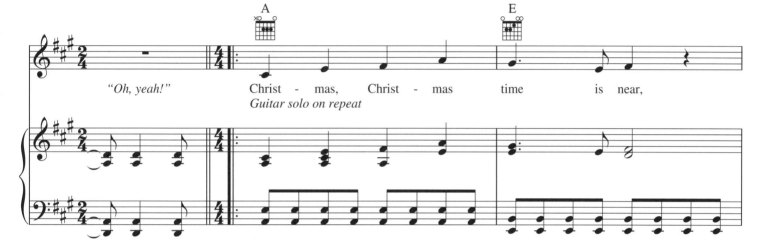

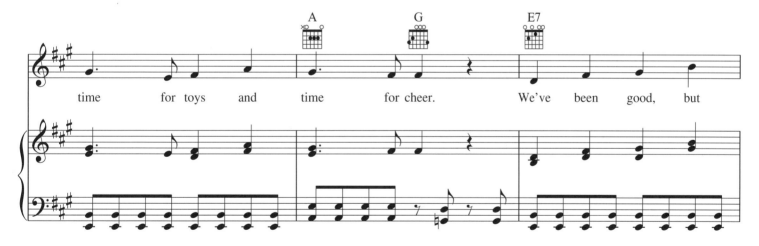

Want a plane that loops the loop; me, I want a

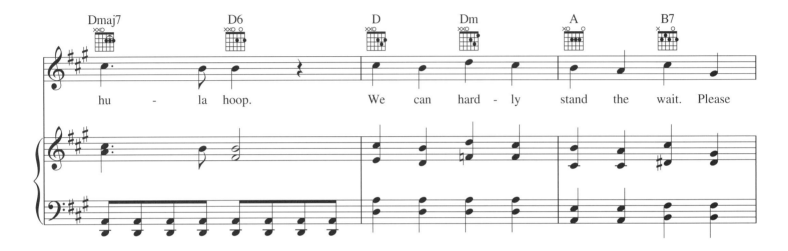

hu - la hoop. We can hard - ly stand the wait. Please

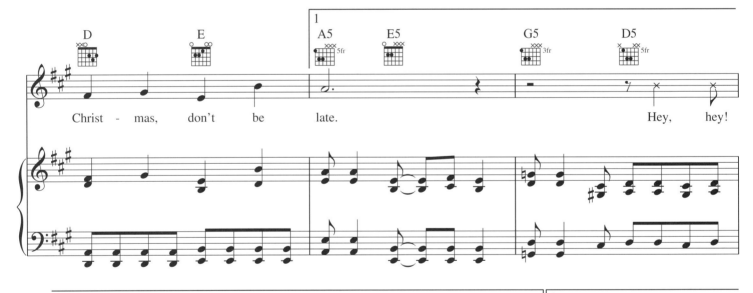

Christ - mas, don't be late. Hey, hey!

Yeah, _____ come on!

we can't last. Hur - ry Christ - mas, hur - ry fast.

Want a plane that loops the loop; me, I want a

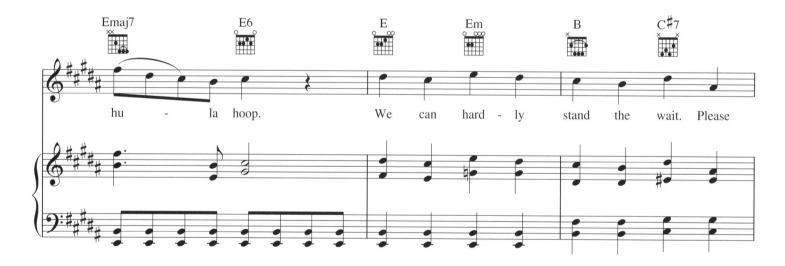

hu - la hoop. We can hard - ly stand the wait. Please

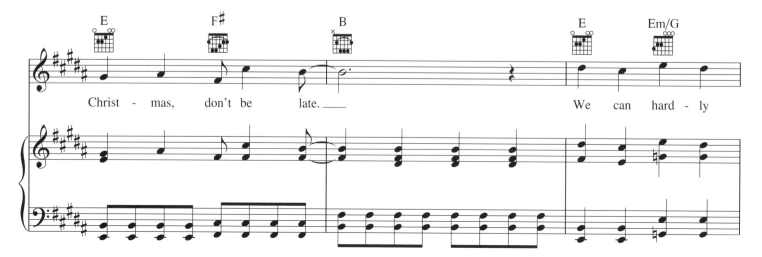

Christ - mas, don't be late. _____ We can hard - ly

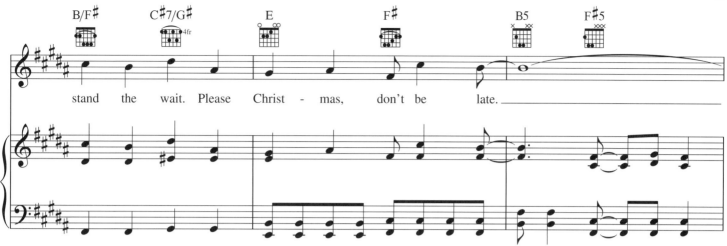

stand the wait. Please Christ - mas, don't be late. _____

_____ Don't be late. _____ Don't be late. _

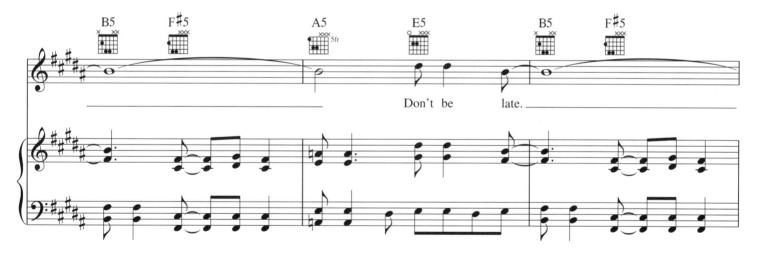

_____ Don't be late. _____

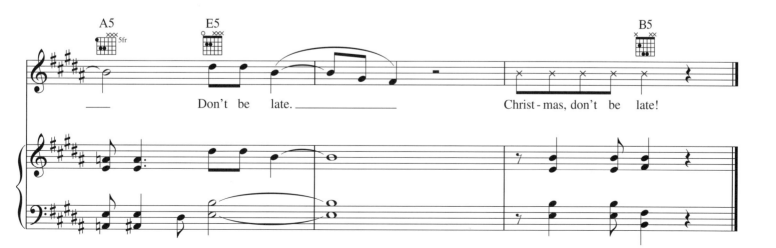

_____ Don't be late. _____ Christ - mas, don't be late!

FUNKYTOWN

Words and Music by
STEVEN GREENBERG

Moderately fast

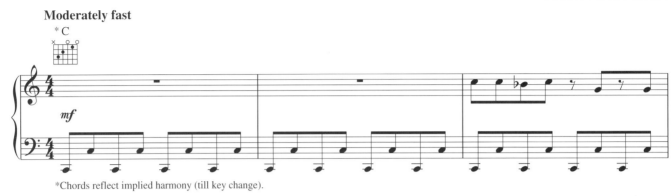

*Chords reflect implied harmony (till key change).

Got -

ta make a move to a town that's right __ for me.

Town __ to keep me mov - in', keep me groov - in' with some en - er - gy.

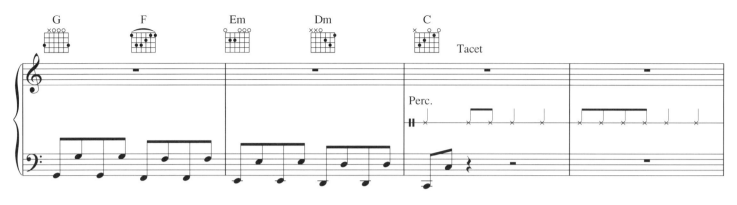

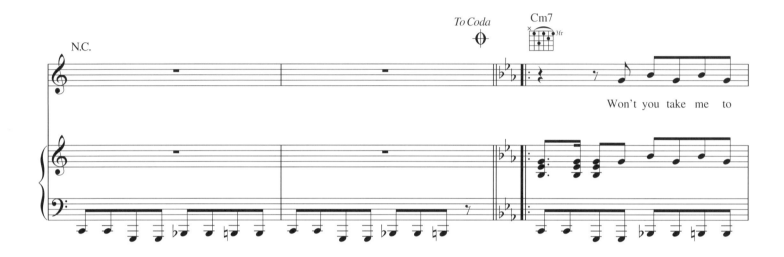

Won't you take me to

Funk - y - town?   Won't you take me to   Funk - y - town?

D.C. (with repeats) al Coda

(Sing 1st time only)

Won't you take me down _____ to Funk - y - town? _____

Repeat and fade

_____ Won't you take me down _____ to Funk - y - town?

GET YOU GOIN'

Words and Music by ALI THEODORE, JOSEPH KATSAROS,
ALANA DAFONSECA and AARON SANDLOFER

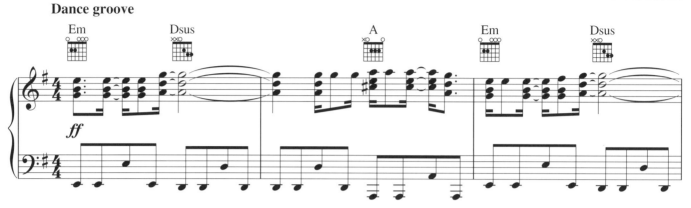

Oh, __ oh, __ oh, __ oh, __ oh, __ oh, __ oh, __ oh. __

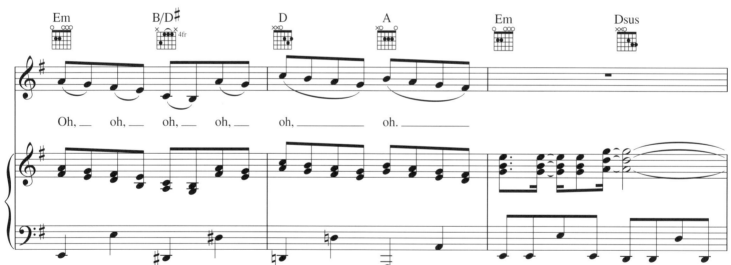

Oh, __ oh, __ oh, __ oh, __ oh, __ oh. __

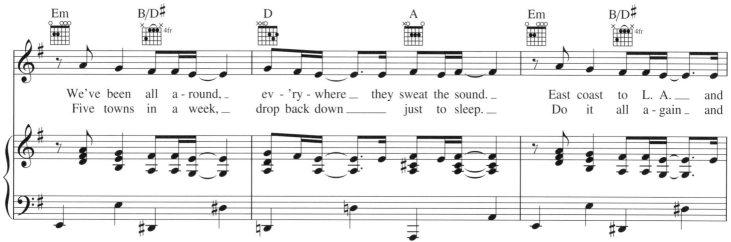

We've been all a - round, __ ev - 'ry - where __ they sweat the sound. __ East coast to L. A. __ and
Five towns in a week, __ drop back down ____ just to sleep. __ Do it all a - gain __ and

all that's on __ the way, __ yeah. __ Don't want flash - y things, __
all be - cause __ of you, __ yeah. __ Three kids on the road, __ from

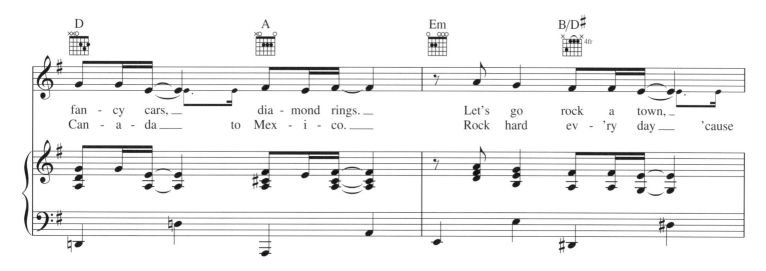

fan - cy cars, __ dia - mond rings. __ Let's go rock a town, __
Can - a - da __ to Mex - i - co. __ Rock hard ev - 'ry day __ 'cause

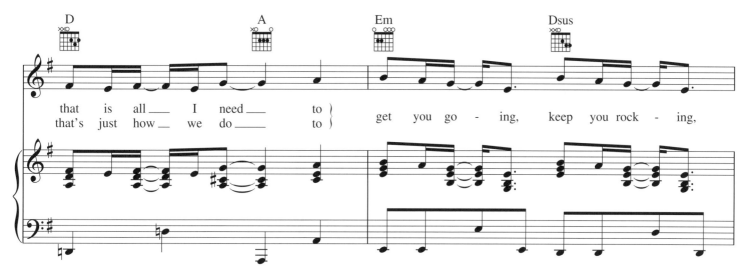

that is all __ I need __ to ⎰ get you go - ing, keep you rock - ing,
that's just how __ we do __ to ⎱

start the par - ty, nev - er stop - ping. Get you mov - ing, get you sing - ing,

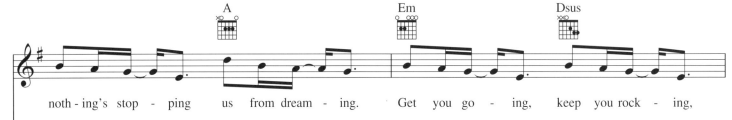

noth - ing's stop - ping us from dream - ing. Get you go - ing, keep you rock - ing,

start the par - ty, nev - er stop - ping. Get you mov - ing, get you sing - ing,

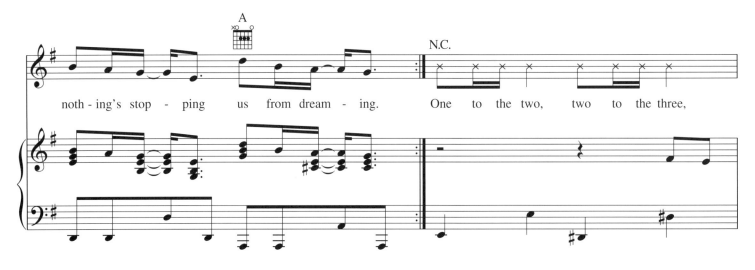

noth - ing's stop - ping us from dream - ing. One to the two, two to the three,

Get you go - ing, keep you rock - ing, start the par - ty, nev - er stop - ping.

Get you mov - ing, get you sing - ing, noth - ing's stop - ping us from dream - ing.

Get you go - ing, keep you rock - ing, start the par - ty, nev - er stop - ping.

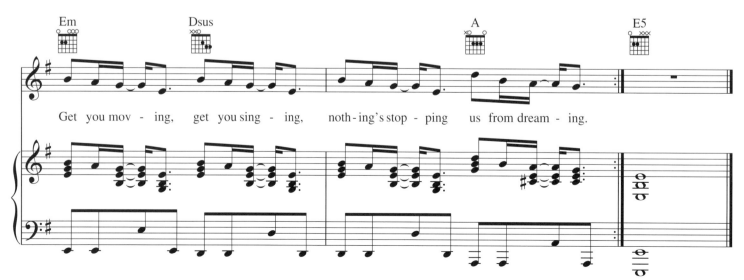

Get you mov - ing, get you sing - ing, noth - ing's stop - ping us from dream - ing.

COAST 2 COAST

Words and Music by ALI THEODORE,
ZACH DANZIGER, ALANA DAFONSECA,
VINCENT T. ALFIERI and JULIAN DAVIS

Fast Rock

Lyrics:

I've been to Al - a - bam - a,
I'm liv - ing like a star

I've been to Ten - nes - see,
out in Hol - ly - wood.

I did a show ___ at the
Next ___ day we hit New

Al - a - mo ___ last week.
York and it's ___ all good.

And in Lou - i - si - an - a,
I'm in Chi - ca - go. I see

I met An - na and her friend. She said, "You come in town, I'll
Mar - go, I say ba - by, hey. In Col - o - ra - do by to -

hang a - round with you a - gain." Hey, li'l dar - ling, let me
mor - row, 'noth - er gig to play. Ev - 'ry time we jam, ___ got a

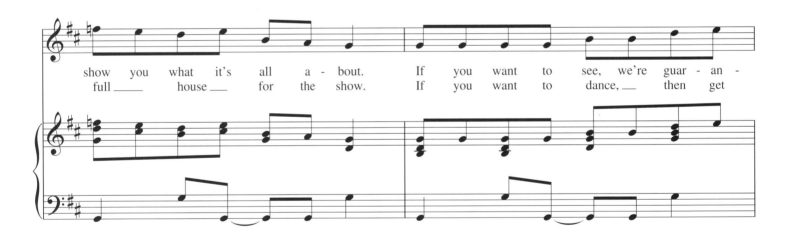

show you what it's all a - bout. If you want to see, we're guar - an -
full ___ house ___ for the show. If you want to dance, ___ then get

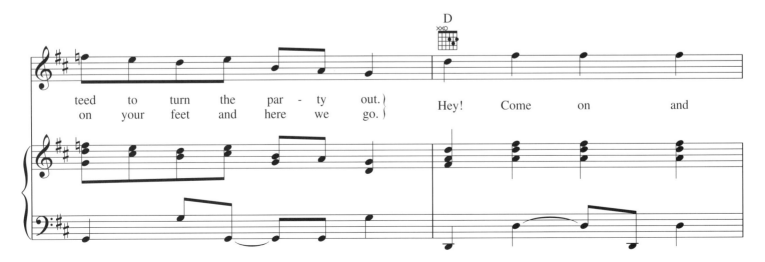

teed to turn the par - ty out. Hey! Come on and
on your feet and here we go. }

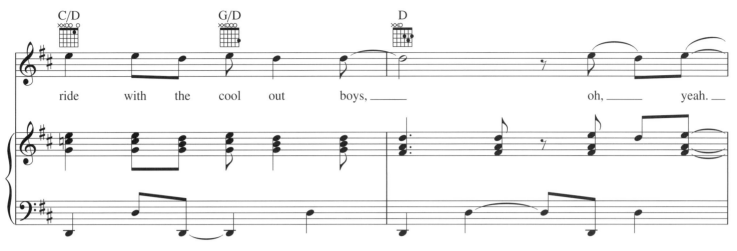

ride with the cool out boys, _____ oh, _____ yeah. _____

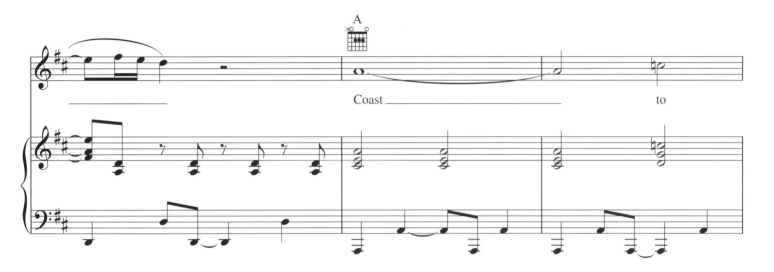

_____ Coast _____ to

coast, we're on ___ the road. ___ Ev - 'ry - bod - y got - ta

make some noise, _ get down in the town with them Chip - munk boys. _ They're

on the road ___ liv- ing out their dreams. ___ If you love them, real- ly love them, let me

hear y'all scream. ___ Take a step to the left, then slide to the right.

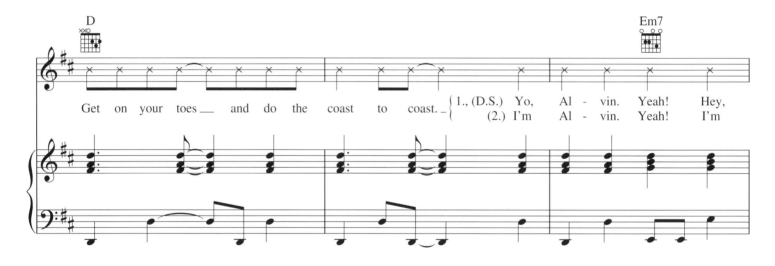

Get on your toes ___ and do the coast to coast. ___ {1., (D.S.) Yo, Al - vin. Yeah! Hey,
                                                      (2.) I'm Al - vin. Yeah! I'm

Si - mon. Yeah! Yo, The - o - dore. Yeah! We're the Chip - munks!
Si - mon. Yeah! I'm The - o - dore. Yeah! We're the Chip - munks!

ONLY YOU
(And You Alone)

Words and Music by BUCK RAM
and ANDE RAND

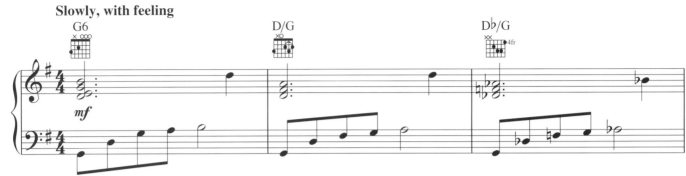

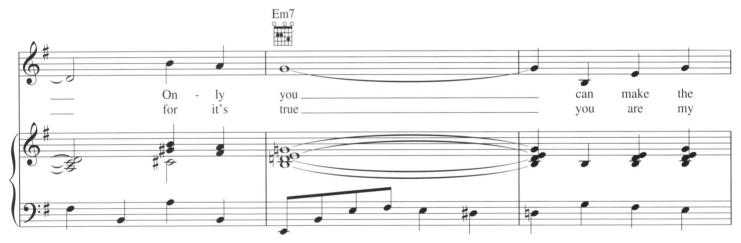

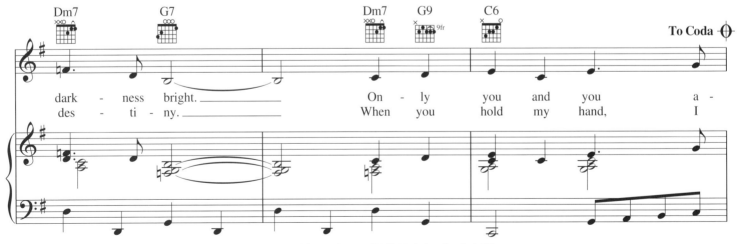

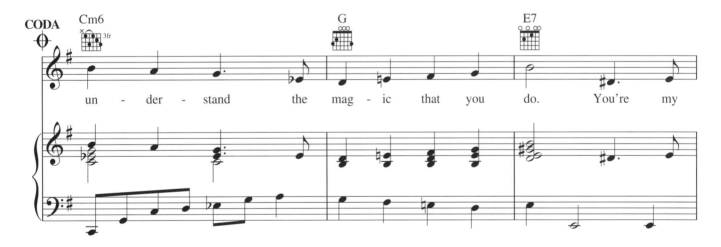

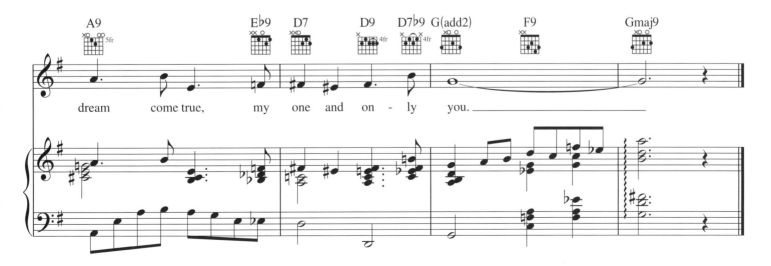

MESS AROUND

Words and Music by ALI THEODORE,
ALANA DAFONSECA and AARON SANDLOFER

Quick R&B

Oh, yeah. Come on, ___ now. Chip - munks,

bring-in' it back. It's been a long time, it's been a hard road,

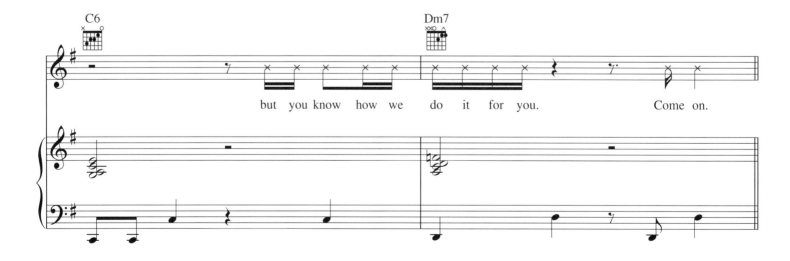

but you know how we do it for you. Come on.

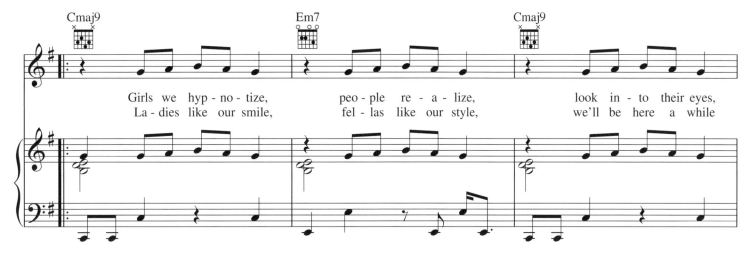

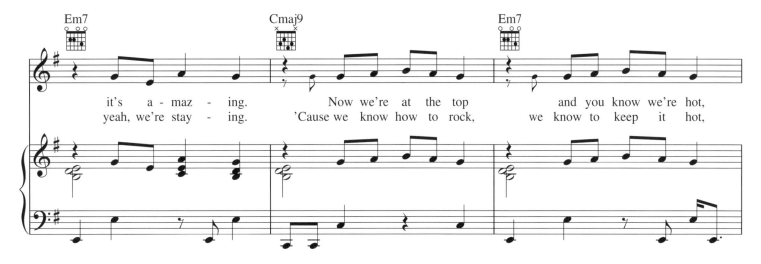

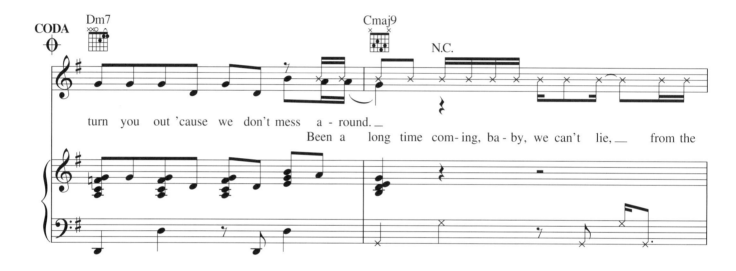

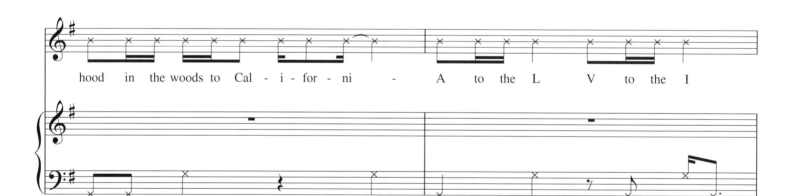

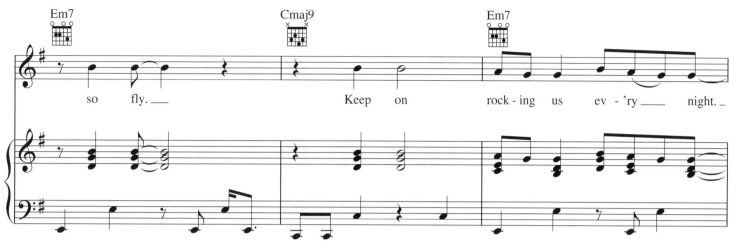

so fly. ___ Keep on rock - ing us ev - 'ry ___ night. ___

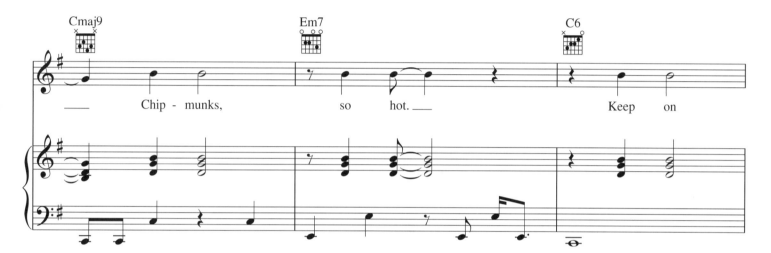

___ Chip - munks, so hot. ___ Keep on

keep - ing on, nev - er ___ stop. It's been a long time com - ing and we're

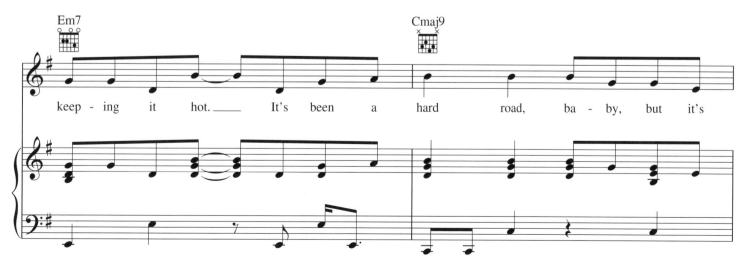

keep - ing it hot. ___ It's been a hard road, ba - by, but it's

worth it. We work it all in the club, on the road. It's been tough, but you know ___ we keep it

go - ing for you now. Yeah, turn you out 'cause we don't mess a - round. ___

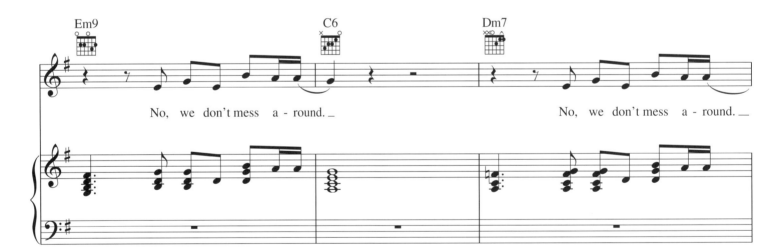

No, we don't mess a - round. ___ No, we don't mess a - round. ___

No, we don't mess a - round. ___

AIN'T NO PARTY

Words and Music by ALI THEODORE,
ZACH DANZIGER and JULIAN DAVIS

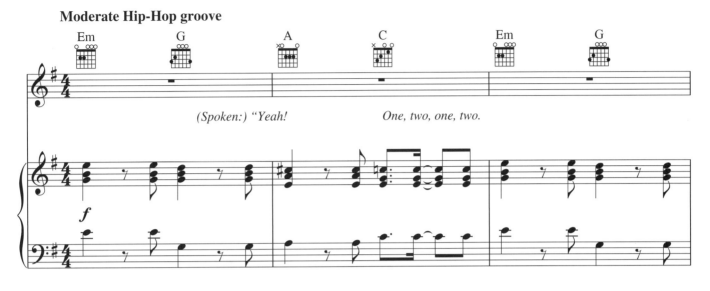

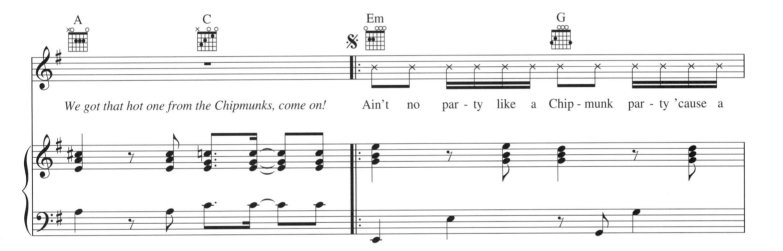

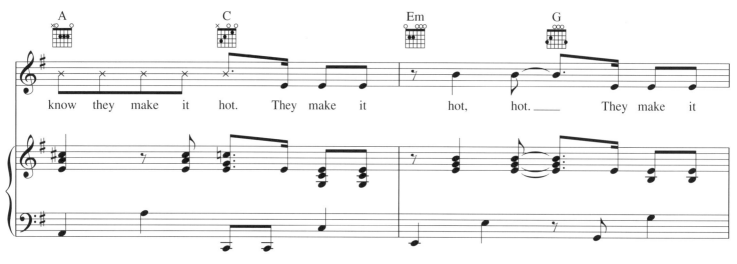

know they make it hot. They make it hot, hot. ___ They make it

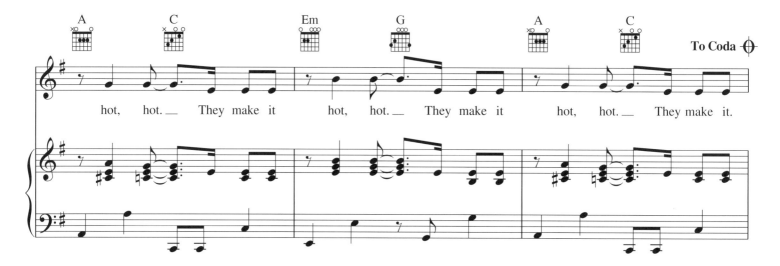

To Coda ⊕

hot, hot. ___ They make it hot, hot. ___ They make it hot, hot. ___ They make it.

N.C.

Step in - side the par - ty, y'all know our name. ___ Pa - pa - raz - zi out - side glad we came. ___ Got to
We go where we want to go, flow how we want to flow. If you don't _ know, well, now you know. _

take some pho - tos with a cou - ple of fans. ___ If you don't show love they won't be in the stands. ___
Hav - in' a good _ time is what _ we're af - ter, ___ chill - ing with friends for ___ fun ___ and laugh - ter.

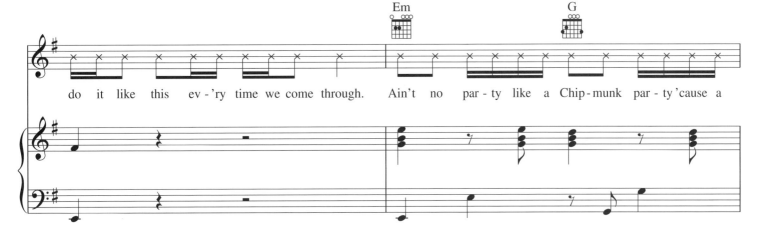

do it like this ev-'ry time we come through. Ain't no par-ty like a Chip-munk par-ty 'cause a

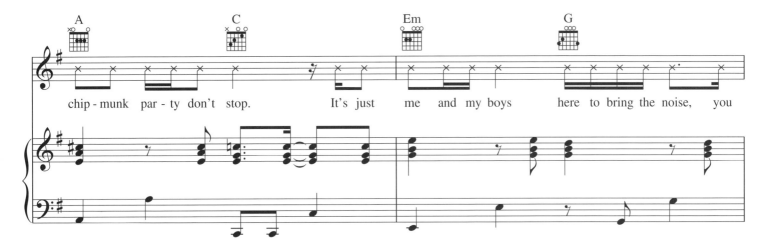

chip-munk par-ty don't stop. It's just me and my boys here to bring the noise, you

know they make it hot. They make it hot, hot. __ They make it hot, hot. __ They make it

hot, hot. __ They make it hot, hot. __ They make it hot.

GET MUNK'D

Words and Music by ALI THEODORE,
JOSEPH KATSAROS, ZACH DANZIGER,
ALANA DAFONSECA and VINCENT T. ALFIERI

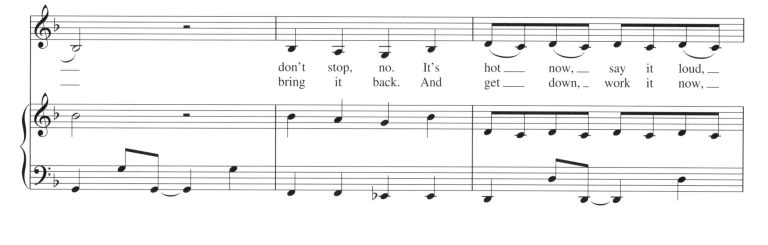

Yeah, boy, I think I'm fall-ing. I got you beg-ging, "Please." _ I got to have you, ba-by.

I'm gon-na get you, girl. Yeah, boy, I might go cra-zy. Rock your world. _____

Get Munk'd, _ the Chip-munks al-ways gon-na get _____ bumped. _ Don't

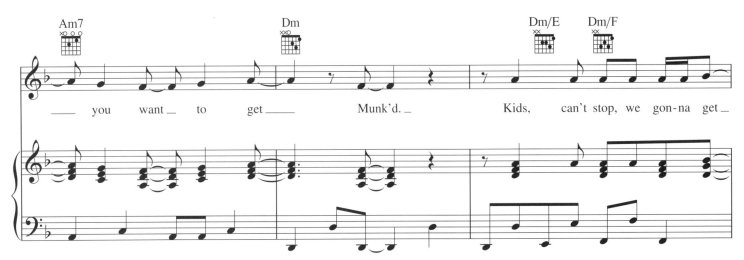

_____ you want _ to get _____ Munk'd. _ Kids, can't stop, we gon-na get _